ENLIGHTEN THE SELF

REALISE AND CONNECT

With The Natural

ENLIGHTEN THE SELF REALISE AND CONNECT

With The Natural

BALESHWAR PUROHIT

ZORBA BOOKS

ZORBA BOOKS

Publishing Services by Zorba Books, December 2019

Website: www.zorbabooks.com
Email: info@zorbabooks.com

Cover design© Sithesh

ISBN Print Book - 978-81-943110-9-6
ISBN eBook – 978-93-88497-96-1

Zorba Books Pvt. Ltd. (opc)
Sushant Arcade,
Next to Courtyard Marriot,
Sushant Lok 1, Gurgaon – 122009, India

DEDICATION

I dedicate this book to my mother Srimati Raksha Purohit and to my father Shri Ramesh Purohit for their affection, blessings, guidance, kind cooperation & for showing the direction towards positivity, social service, introspection, acceptance & subsequent improvement of the self, by the self which helped me to create the contents of this book.

To my cousins Late Pallavi Sharma and Late Nagender Vyas.

To Mother Earth and all the powers which exist in the limitless and the infinite.

ACKNOWLEDGEMENTS

Gratitude is a blessing in itself. It is because of introspection and realization of the self, by the self and gives birth to serenity, a sense of contentment and gratification to the self while emitting good vibrations and demonstrating gratitude during interaction with the living, the non-living and all the powers which exist in the infinite, for the involvement of their indispensable presence.

First and Foremost, I would like to thank the creator who is also called the Almighty, God and the invisible power for making me an instrument to convey to the world the thoughts of the universal mind.

I would like to thank mighty nature and powers which are there for keeping me together (body, mind and soul), giving the ideas and cultivating a different perspective for observation within which assisted me to create the contents of this book.

I would like to thank the persons who have a pure mind & a pure heart, those whose karmas are just like that of Maha-atamas, those who live for & strive to obtain justice for others, serve all beings, those who have devotion towards their Karma and contribute to a change for the positive and take their mind into a healthy dimension, make their surroundings healthy and give a different perspective to the world. In a true sense, they are Yogis by themselves and also to those departed souls who committed themselves towards a change for the positive against all odds, for their positive thoughts and vibrations which assisted me to create the contents of this book.

I would like to thank my parents, cousins, friends, teachers, along with all the others from whom I have learnt about life & many of the faceless millions for giving me affection, prayers, blessings and showering love and understanding on my arduous journey of creating the contents of this book. They are too many to be named here. In retrospect the list seems to be endless.

I would like to especially thank Shri Suprio Ghosh Ji who is a realist, a positive thinker, a poet, a songwriter, a short story writer, a cartoonist and the author of 'How To Stop Wars???','Terror In Our Midst', 'Wake Up Oh! Indian Wake Up Please' and 'Unity In Diversity Can Save Our World' for showering affections, blessings, understanding and writing a foreword and assisting me while I was giving finishing touches to this book.

I would also like to thank Shri Vishal Nanda Ji who is a realist, a positive thinker, a storyteller and a writer for assisting me in proof reading and writing a foreword for this book while showering affections on me.

A NOTE FROM THE POET

The ideas or thoughts which are in this book or the ones I get don't belong to me, since the universal mind and nature always empower & encourage me to pen down their ideas or thoughts in a poetic manner or in other ways. Rather than believing that I'm a poet or a writer and that the ideas originate from me, I accept the truth that I'm an instrument of the universal mind and nature to convey their messages.

Life on Planet Earth is an invaluable gift but it is also a responsibility towards Karma. Karma which is associated with spreading the message of love, unity, serenity and cooperation, while preserving life forms, non-living things and not mis-utilizing or aiding in the destruction of life and resources.

Since life is a priceless gift. Anyone who is a part of this world, that person's existence influences the Global Village as far as other living beings & non-living matter are concerned they influence it as well. One always comes across with millions of people in one's life time and is influenced by the worldly affairs and the environment which is created by their positive and negative vibes. Influenced by the environment either one has a healthy state of mental affairs or takes one's mind into a negative direction.

The present state of affairs of our world is a far cry from what is acceptable. Avarice, gluttony, abhorrence, slander, unachievable, desires, negative affairs, pretentions of knowing it all while knowing a miniscule & the subsequent arrogance & the justifications for blatantly ignoring facts and unjustifiable inactions, is our everyday reality due to this Planet Earth which is a living Planet is becoming unhealthy. Unpredictable, unfathomable disasters & new problems keep arising.

As far as the ecology, the flora & fauna are concerned, rarely anyone thinks about their rights, protection, what they contribute to the world & how precious they are. They too have rights similar to human beings and Planet Earth is their home as well.

The leaders usually mislead the gullible public who feel something is being done but the reality is that only talks are held, promises are pledged, sometimes broken but there is never any subsequent positive action and public wealth is squandered with no positive result or achievement.

The leaders, who are ruling the world, take initiative, organize talks & debate to show the gullible public that they are sorting out the problems which the world is in, so that no one can protest & uproot their governance. After that they divert the public mind space towards other issues. Problems remain as they have been, aggravating, the situation becomes from bad to worse. The persons who expose the intricacies behind the scene are pressurized, ignored, sidelined or sometimes massacred. It clearly indicates that most of Planet Earth's citizens are more bothered about name, fame, money, pleasure, power & unachievable desires.

This book is meant to convey to the world the message of Mother Earth and expose the hidden truths which exist. It also shows the beauty of the infinite natural world and is meant to prod one into contemplation about the invisible & hidden powers which are there & the messages that the natural world contains which make the world prosperous, healthy, wealthy, unique, civilized and wonderful. It conveys that realization, introspection, acceptance & the improvement of the self are required to open & conquer one's own mind space. Furthermore, it also encourages one & all to be sane, wise, just, a keen observer & an enlightened being.

It deals with the different realities of the world of today. How justifications without contemplation, realization, introspection & acceptance of learning are ruling the roost and have become a part of the daily norms. How talks about change for the positive take place but the required subsequent actions are ignored.

This book makes a small contribution towards conveying the message of the infinite natural world and Mother Earth so that the world can comprehend the divine harmonious music of nature which is expressed by the natural elements. Moreover, it obliges us to accept the fact that other beings and nature are so priceless and precious, it encourages one to have an un-destructive attitude and create a state of positive mental affairs to convert our reality into a dimension that is just, sane, wise, reasonable and civilized. Since realization, introspection, acceptance & self improvement help in conquering & opening-up one's mind space that's why the change for the positive is achievable. It also discloses that changing one's own self helps to change the vibrations of the surrounding world or takes the world into a dimension which is filled with love, happiness, serenity, joy, prosperity & positivity.

It also conveys to the world the awakening call of Mother Earth and all the powers that exist within the limitless which the world ought to perceive in a realistic manner so that the world can comprehend the true worth of life force and be receptive to positive thoughts, energy & feel the truth of our reality. The world ought not do any harm to any being and ought to respect them and spread affection, kindness, serenity and joy to each & every being's life. The world ought to rectify the problems which exist in our Global Village. Since love, unity & cooperation cures any type of problem therefore the world ought to be united, have a unity of purpose & cooperation and not be self centric with ulterior motives and adhere to the standards while curing them.

Baleshwar Purohit

FOREWORD (1)

Thoughts dominate the mind thus the being. Since thoughts lead to actions subsequent actions no matter how insignificant affect us all.

Thinking restricted by community traditions & mass views along with avarice for material benefits & the quest for overnight success seems to have become the way of the world of today.

Exceptions aside negative thought patterns rule the day.

Man has been blinded by desire.

In the process man has not only over-utilized and over–exploited natural resources with total disregard for nature but mis-utilized them to the extent that unfathomable disasters lie around the corner. Some have already started taking place like melting of the poles & glaciers and associated disasters. There are many more waiting to happen.

Nature has variety beyond imagination & is bountiful. It is a fact which we are all aware of, though at the same time we ignore a basic truth. A very important truth.

The truth states that nature provides more than enough for each & every living being's need. But nature doesn't provide enough for anyone's greed.

Ignoring this truth has upset the natural balance.

Since ages Planet Earth has been slowly & steadily heading towards destruction & demise. Accelerating pace with the industrial revolution to the state of affairs of Planet Earth of today, wherein scientists predict that different types of catastrophic disasters will happen in the near future between 2025 and 2040, changing the world the way we know it forever.

If we claim to be evolved & civilized we ought to imbibe positive thinking.

Doing so is urgent.

The state of affairs of Planet Earth is no longer healthy and is deteriorating at an alarming pace.

Millions are squandered in international conferences with insignificant outcome.

The poet tries to awaken and assist the reader to go out of the stereo type mindset of today and realise our reality.

That Planet Earth is a living Planet. That Planet Earth nurtures us all.

Every living being has a soul, feelings and a unique way to convey thoughts.

The poet truly believes that he is an instrument of the universal mind and nature to spread positive thoughts & energy and to enlighten fellow beings about our reality so that we stop harming nature and eventually reverse the damage that has already been done.

SUPRIO GHOSH

THE SECOND OF NOVEMBER, 2019

FOREWORD (2)

During such times when mankind is so busy with the destruction of all life, This book is an attempt full of wishes and blessings, wishes that all mankind has had during childhood but forgotten over ages: to live in peace and harmony a beautiful life of happiness and prosperity to produce a healthy and civilized world.

The book tells us, rather reminds us, of all the high virtues of Mother Earth and life in general to help us grow ourselves and live with Nature in harmony. It calls for a holistic improvement of our behavior for a healthier state of mind that is away from negativity, ignorance and greed.

Humans are devoted beings by nature and the author is making an effort to guide us into a direction, where devotion towards preserving Nature in its various forms can help us awaken to realize a better and wholesome life.

Life is a blessing and a gift, when appreciated it brings abundance of all good things, but if humans keep disregarding the blessings of Mother Earth, the Universe and everything natural then it will soon be reduced to a ruined state of being.

If the ideas and thoughts in this book are understood genuinely then positive change is not a farfetched reality, it wants to encourage and emphasize positivity and simple wisdom to attain the necessary will that brings about a reform that humanity has always dreamt of: which is to value and cherish the grace of the Almighty.

VISHAL NANDA

THE SIXTH OF NOVEMBER, 2019

CONTENTS

1. THE TREE...23

2. THE MOUNTAINS...29

3. NATURE...33

4. WHO GETS BLESSINGS FROM THE NATURAL JEWELS?..35

5. THE PRESENT REALITY OF THE WORLD...................39

6. A CALL OF THE INFINITE NATURAL WORLD...........41

7. LOOK AT..43

8. A SCENE OF JOY & ENLIGHTENMENT.....................45

9. THE RIVER..47

10. THE QUESTIONS RAISED BY OTHER BEINGS...........49

11. THE TREE IS NOT ONLY A TREE...............................51

12. THE SUN...57

13. THE WATERFALLS...59

14. THE MOON..61

15. OH! BOUNDLESS SKY...63

16. NATURE..65

17. A WELCOMING CALL...69

18. AN INDICATION..71

19. THE FLOWERS...73

20. THE NATURAL URGES..75

21. I'M A TREE..77

22. THE SNOWFALL..79

23. A DAY OF THE NATURAL WORLD............................81

24. AN ENLIGHTENING MESSAGE OF THE NATURAL
    JEWELS...83

25. THE SPRING SEASON..85

26. APPROACHING SUMMER....................................87

27. THE SUMMER SEASON.......................................89

28. EARLY RAINS...91

29. THE RAINY SEASON...93

30. AN INVITATION OF AUTUMN..............................95

31. OH! WINTER...97

32. THE VOICE OF NATURE.....................................99

33. THE WISDOM OF A MOONLIT NIGHT....................101

34. THE ENLIGHTENING MESSAGE OF MOTHER
    EARTH..103

35. A CALL OF THE NATURAL JEWELS......................105

36. I'M EARTH..107

37. THE MESSAGE OF THE NATURAL WORLD.............109

38. AN AWAKENING CALL......................................113

39. THE WORLD OF TODAY....................................115

40. WHY???..117

41. THE VOICE OF OTHER BEINGS................................121

42. OH! DEAR CHILDREN................................123

43. LET'S DO IT TODAY & NOW................................127

44. OH! MY DEAR CHILDREN................................129

45. THE SAYINGS OF THE WISE PEOPLE................................131

46. THE SORROW OF THE NATURAL WORLD AND
    WISE CALLING................................133

47. RESPECT................................135

48. WATER, THE PRICELESS RESOURCE................................137

49. INTROSPECT................................141

50. SAVE WATER, SAVE LIFE................................143

51. THE MESSAGE FROM THE NATURAL................................145

52. THE CALL OF NATURE................................147

53. LET'S UNITE................................149

54. UNITY & CO-OPERATION................................151

55. GIVE A HAND................................153

56. I, I, I & I................................155

Oh !
Love Spread
Love

1. THE TREE

The leaves of the trees move happily
When the gentle breeze blows
With new hopes
Similar to a river, within it life energy flows

The song of brotherhood, companionship & love
The tree always sings
An intimate connection
Exists among the trees and all beings

This relationship
Has no end
And the tree is not a foe
But a true friend

The trees and plants are like donors
They give the world herbs, flowers and fruits
Many creatures hum a harmonious chant, while on the trees
It seems as though they play musical instruments, especially flutes

Trees have different colours in different seasons

During the gentle breeze and windstorms, they dance like peacocks

They give the world shade, wood, food and oxygen

They have many varieties like firs, pines, deodars and oaks

In this world, the objective of the tree, is to serve the world

To accomplish the task of the invisible power is the tree's duty

The trees are a symbol of peace, love, wisdom & security

Along with prosperity, responsibility, sacrifice, and beauty

The souls of living beings

Live within the emotions of the trees

The tree is a beautiful creation of the unknown entities

But it depends on what one observes, what one sees

The tree assists to enhance

Mother Earth's sheen

The tree makes the atmosphere

Healthy and clean

The trees always convey to the world

Don't do vicious deeds, become kind & mild

Trees create a conducive environment

And a tree is Mother Earth's child

The trees are worshiped as Gods or Goddesses

The trees are a source of cheerfulness

On the other hand

Sometimes the trees are cut down due to greed and selfishness

The world ought not forget the value of the trees

And ought to follow the loving message which the trees impart

The trees are an invaluable gift to the world

And their surroundings soothe each & every being's heart

The world must introspect and contemplate

They ought not be cut down for any unjustifiable reason

The world must plant and protect trees

So that trees will be there in each and every season

Laws exist and are implemented for human beings

Some laws are meant for the plants, the trees & any other being

But are rarely enforced and not strictly adhered to

New laws & actions are required which the songs of equality sing

Every being which exists, has equal rights to live & play

It's the universal will & an awakening call

The world ought to create & enforce new laws

Not only for human beings but those which are for one & all

2. THE MOUNTAINS

The mountains have diversity and are enormous
The hidden truths of nature, they always preserve & know
The mountains are so precious
And their peaks are clothed with snow

In the vastness of the mountains
Uncountable living beings nurture & grow
Even though the lava erupts from the craters
Every mountain is a friend, not a foe

The river starts its journey
At the mountains' feet
Like pearls, the peaks of mountains glow
In the bright Sun's heat

The mountains give the world
Indispensable things
The songs of prosperity, freshness, calmness, unity & brotherhood
Every mountain always sings

In the spring season

The mountains appear with new life-forms & fondness

In the summer season

The mountains are conveniently cool & full of freshness

In the rainy season

The mountains are lush green

In the winter season

The mountains are frozen, bright & clean

The animals & birds

The forests and the trees

The snow and the rivers

The mist and the breeze

The flowers and the grass

The waterfalls & the natural fountains

The bushes and the rocks

Enhance the exquisiteness of the mountains

The world begets from the mountains
Knowledge, wisdom, imagination, wealth & treasure
Power, strength, courage, potential & compassion
Love, peace, happiness, enlightenment and pleasure

Every action of the world
The mountains always see
Since ages, the mountains have been protecting
And nourishing the world like a tree

3. NATURE

Nature gives everyone an embrace

Nature is a beautiful creation of the Almighty

Nature nourishes the world

Nature is mighty

Nature imparts to the world love and sunshine

Nature is blessed by the invisible deity

Nature imparts to everyone serenity and newness

Nature has a glorious sheen

Everyday nature comes with a different pose

Nature has different hues of green

Nature conveys one & all to respect everyone

Nature is blissful, cool & keen

Nature encourages everyone to spread goodwill

Nature in itself is change

Nature reveals the truths of the world

Nature has an infinite range

Nature conveys to everyone

Introspect & seek within the self, the strange

Nature heals every beings strain, stress & strife

Nature shows the path of introspection

Nature makes the world prosperous and bright

From different perspectives, nature expresses her love & affection

Nature gives the world indispensable things

Nature takes everyone into a new dimension

Nature enlightens everyone

Nature helps each & every being to open one's mind

But devilish ulterior motives hidden deep in man's mind space

Makes him commit evil acts and be unjust, vicious and unkind

In spite of this

Nature is so caring and kind

4. WHO GETS BLESSINGS FROM THE NATURAL JEWELS?

Those who believe in themselves

While in difficult times

Those who never lose their confidence

And the sense of responsibility

The winds assist them

Those who live for others

Be positive

Never give up and are tolerant

And diminish cruelty

The powers derived from the rays of the Sun are with them

Those who learn from their own errors

And realize that time is a precious gift

Those who utilize it for good purposes

And to improve their abilities and capabilities

Time respects them

Those who seek knowledge & wisdom

Expose the realities that engulf our world

Pay reverence to each and every being

And spread happiness, kindness and serenity

The flow of the water is with them

Those who turn the world into a beautiful place

And are dedicated towards their karma

Those who have love for beauty and nature

And serve all beings

The clouds bow in front of them

Those who give everyone

Respect and affection

Those who spread the message of love, harmony & friendship

And abstain from inanity & insanity

Nature adores them

5. THE PRESENT REALITY OF THE WORLD

The domination games are going on

Unique native & exotic creatures are vanishing

The lands of other beings are being occupied

Terrible diseases are emerging

Terrorism is tumefying

Pollution and contamination are increasing

Excessive mining is going on

The forests are diminishing or decreasing

The sky is smoggy

The rivers, the lakes, the seas & the oceans are being polluted

Heaps of plastic waste and garbage are in every nook & corner

Natural resources are being looted

Innocent, other beings are being massacred

The trees are being cut down

Immense buildings and roads are engulfing the natural

The forests are turning into a big city or a town

Nature is being contaminated

Respect for beauty and nature rarely one can trace

Negative thoughts are ruling the roost

Only talks about change for the positive take place

Like Global warming, depleting drinking water and more

New problems are rising & the situation is so tense

The mountains are being broken down

The villages, the cities and the towns are becoming dense

The climate is changing

People are forgetting & rarely any one cares

The value of nature, creatures, love, respect and brotherhood

Due to rapacity, un-gettable longings & a state of negative affairs

6. A CALL OF THE INFINITE NATURAL WORLD

Don't kill animals and birds

Don't incarcerate them in the cages

Don't throw stones at them

Don't hunt them and make it a part of your entertainment

Don't occupy and destroy their homes

Don't disturb them and interfere with their lives

Let them live the way the universal powers desired

Don't pollute and poison

The rivers, the seas, the sky & the oceans

Don't cut down, pollute and poison

The mountains, the plains & fertile soil

Clean them and let them be there as they are

Don't cut the trees

Don't pluck flowers

Don't disturb them

Cause within them life energy flows

The path of positive growth they always show

Let them spread

The fragrance and positive energy which they keep

Don't use natural resources extensively

Utilize them wisely

Don't make lethal weapons and bombs

They only create destruction and demise

Don't be avarice, cruel, insane, unkind and self centric

Don't do horrendous deeds

Don't destroy this planet

Be sane, wise and just

And save this planet

For the next generations to come

So, please save it, save it, save it.............

7. LOOK AT

Look at the trees and the flowers

Receive the tranquility, freshness & the fragrance they impart

Look at the rivers, the mountains, the forests and the plains

Feel the beauty and happiness in your heart

Look at the mist, the rain, snow and hail

Feel the coolness and newness that they spread

Look at the crops, the leaves & the bushes when they sway

Observe the calmness and splendor that they spread

Look at nature

Get enlightenment, confidence, courage, strength & grace

Look at the lakes, waterfalls, volcanoes & rivulets

Them, in your mind space, you ought to embrace

Look at natural marvelous sights

Feel the happiness, harmony & love they bring

Look at unique native & exotic creatures

Listen to the melodious songs they sing

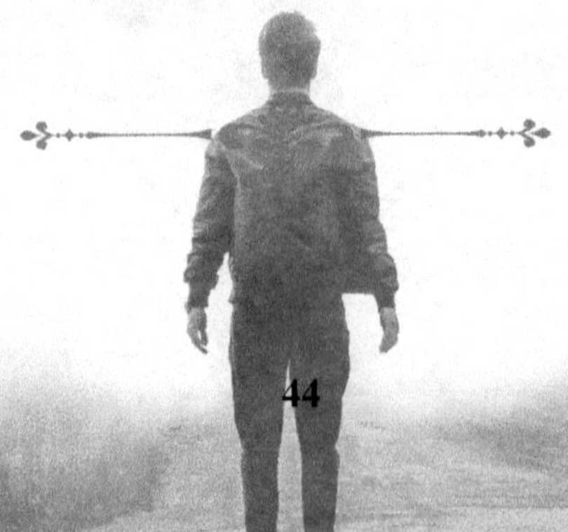

Look at your impulses & actions

Introspect, rectify your fallacies & errors, to cleanse yourself

Look into your own character & judge

Are you always yourself?

Look at the sun, the moon and the stars

Respect each & every being with delight

Look at Mother Earth

Be receptive to positive vibes, patience, kindness & justifiable might

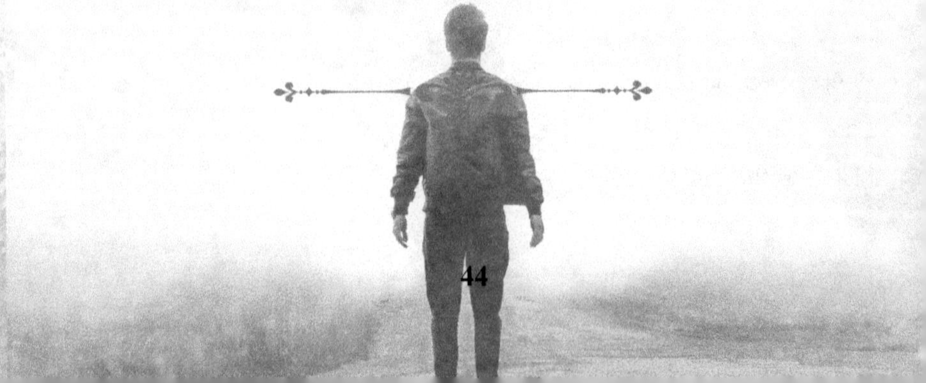

8. A SCENE OF JOY & ENLIGHTENMENT

A magnificent scene

Nature is making

After a wonderful sleep

Human beings are awakening

In every nook & corner

A sweet fragrance of flowers is reaching

A new lesson of acceptance

Nature is teaching

A melodious song

Nature is singing

With full enthusiasm

Nature inconstant motion is swinging

The wind is blowing

And the river is flowing

The mountain peaks are glowing

Each one is reaping whatever one is sowing

Because of this

Everyone is getting strength, joy & freshness

A new day has begun

Spreading the vibrations of happiness

To attain love, serenity, sweetness and newness

Nature is calling

Why is man not accepting the inevitable?

To be one with nature, why is man stalling?

9. THE RIVER

With a melodious sound

Within any mountain's heart

With joyous

The journey of all rivers start

Through beautiful places the river passes

Like the valleys, the forests, the rifts, villages and towns

In the sunlight & the moonlight

The river shines like 'Spiritual crowns'

The river serves the world

Without taking any break

When it flows through different places

It imparts pleasantness for all beings to take

Within the river

A universe lives

Love, happiness, prosperity, tranquillity and strength

The river gives

During the river's journey
The river makes a beautiful scenery
Everywhere in this world
The river assists to enhance Mother Earth's greenery

The river flows
With a different grace
During every season
The river has a different face

When the river joins the ocean
The river gets bliss
The union of the river & the ocean
Is just like a merging kiss

The river is mighty
And the river is prime
The river shows the world
The importance of time

Let's unite
To keep our rivers clean
Let's not filthy our rivers
And maintain each and every river's sheen

10. THE QUESTIONS RAISED BY OTHER BEINGS

Mother Earth gives all beings

All the things they need

Why do human beings hurt her?

Is it due to unnecessary and unacceptable greed?

Mother Earth always spreads love and happiness

In each and every being's life

In the Blue Planet

Why do human beings strive to create destruction and strife?

Nature's priceless gifts like the mountains, the rivers & clouds

Make a fascinating dream like scenery

For their own benefits and accomplishment of desires

Why do human beings destroy greenery?

Mother Earth is in pains

To see the state of affairs, of this inhuman mentality

Why do human beings compulsively hurt other beings?

Why do human beings become a part & parcel of such cruelty?

Mother Earth tells the world

Love and respect each and every plant & creature

On the other hand

Why do human beings destroy & deface nature?

Human beings usually ignore their responsibilities

And what Mother Earth conveys

Human beings usually strive to incarcerate or hurt

Mother Earth's children in so many ways

Human beings ought to brood over these facts

And not from their own distortion and fallacies hide

Otherwise, the beauty, the greenery & the diversity of life

Will not be far and wide

11. THE TREE IS NOT ONLY A TREE

All beings are unique, look at their lives

The tree reduces their strains, stresses and strifes

The tree gives the world a new sheen

The tree makes Mother 'TELLUS' green

Every tree is like you and me

The tree is not only a tree

The tree fulfils the world's needs

The tree always beholds every mortal's deeds

Conveys a message, to serve & protect those who're in pain

To be honest and responsible and not to be insane

Every tree is like you and me

The tree is not only a tree

The trees have many verities and sizes

One notices them when the sun rises

Birds always chirp melodiously around the trees

To know the self, Introspection & acceptance are some of the keys

Every tree is like you and me

The tree is not only a tree

It seems as though the actions of human beings are shoddy

All components of nature are just like Mother Earth's body

The tree is a blessing for all beings because it contributes, still lives

Feel the freshness and happiness that the tree gives

Every tree is like you and me

The tree is not only a tree

Feel the energy that the trees impart

Feel the beauty that touches each and every being's heart

The tree imparts fragrance through its leaves & each and every flower

The tree is one of the unique creations of the universal power

Every tree is like you and me

The tree is not only a tree

The tree serves the world 24 x7

The tree makes Mother 'TELLUS' a real heaven

During snowy winter, the tree appears so white

During spring and rainy spells, green trees are a marvellous sight

Every tree is like you and me

The tree is not only a tree

The tree is the blue planet's soul

During autumn, the leaves of the trees fall

Feel the love that the trees spread and listen to its loving call

It's not only for me; it's for one and all

Every tree is like you and me

The tree is not only a tree

Existence is not possible without life giving nature & the tree

They always help the Global Village & spread happiness & glee

Whereas due to unfathomable desires & a state of negative affairs

Natural places are being looted, polluted & rarely anyone cares

Every tree is like you and me

The tree is not only a tree

Mother Earth is slowly & steadily losing her greenery

Man's avarice & despicable actions, destroys the ambient scenery

And human beings dump heaps of garbage on Mother Earth's face

That is why soon there will be, of plants and trees no trace

Every tree is like you and me

The tree is not only a tree

The trees are being cut extensively with zest

The world is becoming a concrete forest

The forests are no longer dense

Thus the over all situation is very tense

Every tree is like you and me

The tree is not only a tree

The chaotic state of affairs, the world of today is in
Everyone ought to comprehend its reality or else it's a sin
To counter this, start doing acts
The world ought not forget & ignore such facts
Every tree is like you and me
The tree is not only a tree

Therefore, the world must be united to grow trees & flowers
The world ought to unite to eradicate destructive evil powers
And turn Mother 'TELLUS' green
Through unity, love and cooperation the world can protect her sheen
Every tree is like you and me
The tree is not only a tree

12. THE SUN

When the sun appears
For every new day, it's a start
Along with hopes, freshness and bliss
Deep within Mother Earth's heart

When the sun's rays arrive at the surface
Melodious sounds, nature commences
In the sunlight
It seems as though Mother Earth dances

The sun is a source of life and regulates time
The sun is a source of pleasure
The sun is the centre of all planets
The sun is Mother Earth's treasure

The sun serves the world
Without taking any rest
With the touch of the sun's gleam
Each little bird chirps in glee in its nest

The sun helps to make the environment

Healthy and green

And when the sun shines

Mother Earth has a glorious sheen

Nature blossoms

In the sun's light

Like pearls, the mountain peaks glow

When the sun is bright

The sun is powerful

The sun has the might to ignite anything

The sun is wonderful

The sun looks like a golden ring

13. THE WATERFALLS

Displaying one of the beauties of nature

Which brings vibrations of joy to all?

To be happy, civil, just & honest during one's life time

Is the waterfall's call

The magnificence of nature

The waterfall enhances

In the sunlight and the moonlight

The waterfall dances

The melodious music

The waterfall hums

When with the surface

The water of the waterfall bumps

On the banks of the waterfalls

Various flowers and plants grow during different seasons

The ambience of the waterfall assists to open one's mind

It gives coolness, vigour & courage to accomplish one's visions

When it collides with the surface, it seems to be milk falling

The waterfall imparts the world positive vibrations & strength

With the touch of the waterfall

One can comprehend about life's depth and length

The waterfall reveals the realities of our natural world

The waterfall comes with various pleasant outlooks

The freshness of the waterfall has the power to heal all beings' woes

The waterfall is a healer and has beauty beyond its looks

14. THE MOON

The moon is a natural satellite
Of Mother Earth
The moon appears along with peace, coolness, serenity & tranquillity
Exhibiting its true worth

The snowy mountains shine
In the moon's gleam
And the rivers keep flowing
When most, living beings are in a dream

In the moonlight, when the wind blows
The dancing leaves of the trees seem to sing
For each and every being
Happiness, love and joy the moon's vibrations bring

The moon adds to the beauty of the panorama

The loveliness of the night, the moon enhances

Feel the freshness and the peacefulness that the moon imparts

Feel the affection & joy the moon emits in each of its stances

The moon always tells everyone

Be calm, positive, and don't be insane

Never give up, keep doing and trying

Because efforts don't go in vain

In front of the world

Each day the moon has a different pose

In the dark

The hidden exquisiteness of nature, the moon shows

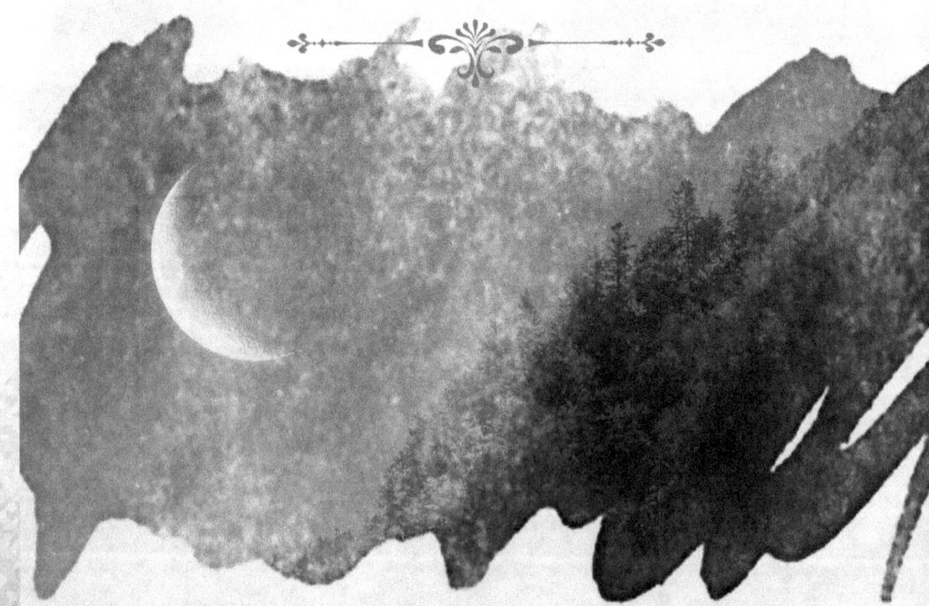

15. OH! BOUNDLESS SKY

Oh! Boundless, Immeasurable sky

You behold us with your hidden eyes

While singing a melodic song of your glory

The birds always enjoy while flying

Through your priceless jewels

The message of love, prosperity, peace & friendship

You spread far and wide

Oh! Boundless, Immeasurable sky

You always appear with a new sheen

The reality about the origin of the universe

You keep and know

You assist to make Mother Earth healthy and green

Your priceless jewels are clouds, rain, mist, hail and snow

When the sound of thunder is very loud

It's like you recite a harmonious song

Oh! Boundless, Immeasurable sky

You enhance the loveliness of Mother Earth's heart

Newness, positivity and good thoughts you always impart

It seems as though you are blue

Every day you come with a different pose

You are wonderful, mighty & an artist

Everyone knows

16. NATURE

Where animals live & play
Where knowledge & wisdom make the day

Where birds fly
Where purity and divine beauty lie

Where the cool breeze blows
Where the river flows

Where precious pearls hide
Where freshness, happiness, and love are far and wide

Where the snow enhances the loveliness
Where the sun and the moon give the power & exquisiteness

Where natural sounds are in a rhyme
Where life has been going on since the beginning of time

Where the trees and the plants dance

Where everyone goes into Shiva's trance

Where mysteries play hide and seek in a flick

Where magic is really magic not a trick

Where the mist, lightening, thunder & clouds make the show

Where all beings know, how to live, love, respect & grow

Wherever happiness, energy & positive vibes one can trace

It happens due to Mother Earth's unending grace

Wherever there is the song of awakening, sung by each creature

They are all part & parcel of kind & mighty nature

17. A WELCOMING CALL

When most beings are in dreams

Millions of stars twinkle in the sky

And appear so bright

Everything is still and calm

Gentle music is in the air

And it echoes to welcome everyone

To observe the beauty of the night

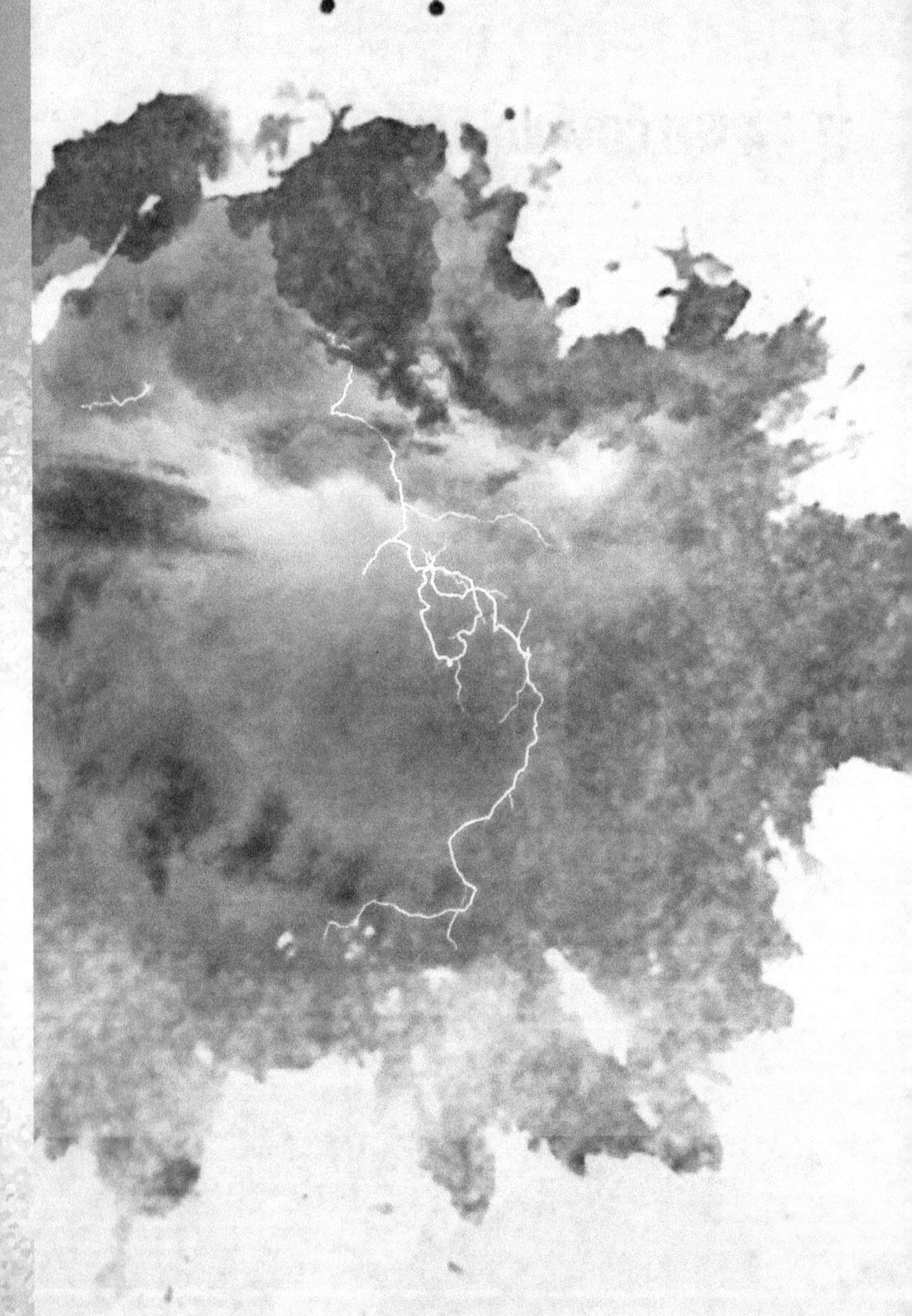

18. AN INDICATION

The sound of thunder

Is very loud

A melody is being sung by

Each and every cloud

The wind blows

Sometimes cool and sometimes warm

As though

It's an alarm of a coming hail storm

19. THE FLOWERS

When the sun shines

The gentle breeze blows

While spreading the fragrance of love, peace, happiness and joy

The flowers blossom & along with them life & positive energy flows

The flowers assist to make Mother Earth

Colorful, beautiful and clean

If one observes, one notices that the flowers sing & dance

And that the flowers are a part of Mother Earth's sheen

When the moon shines at night

There are some sounds of streams

Everything is still and calm

When one has flowers in one's healthy dreams

The flowers enhance the loveliness

The flowers give good sensations

The flowers reduce the negativity

The flowers are one of the most beautiful creations

Do not pluck the flowers

Let them be

Let them spread fragrance & positivity

To know our own selves, let them help you and me

74

20. THE NATURAL URGES

Fifing melodiously

Nature teaches

About this precious life

Nature preaches

Nature gives

Everyone good sensations and strength

Through nature's touch

Everyone comprehends life's depth and length

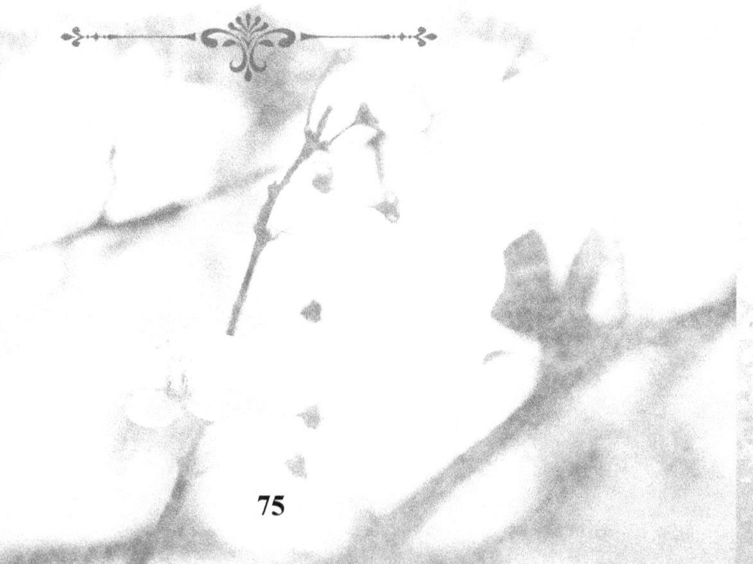

21. I'M A TREE

I keep saying

Utilize me, utilize me

But plant more like me

Take my leaves, cut my branches

For your daily needs

Don't cut me totally

For your avarice & unending desires

My heart is like a sea

I'm a tree

I always assist the world

And show the path

Of introspection, acceptance & self improvement

And spread good vibes & positive energy

On the other hand

The world cuts or hurts or kills me

I'm a tree, I'm a tree

I keep on saying

Save me for the next generations to come

To see Mother Earth

Healthy, prosperous, neat and clean

Plant me, plant me and plant me some-more

And keep her evergreen

22. THE SNOWFALL

Everything is still and calm

When the snow falls

The snow comes with hope, tranquility and joy

To feel the indefinable beauty of nature it always calls

The mist covers the mountains & valleys

When the snowflakes fall from the sky

It seems that Mother Earth is going to wear a white gown

This scene touches you & I

After the snowfall

Serenity & divine beauty are all over the place

And the children play with snow

The environment helps to open one's mind space

Green grass hides beneath the layers of snow

When the fog & the mist disappear

Blocked road, frozen water streams, and lakes

Ladened with snow, the mountains, the trees & the hills appear

The gardens, the roofs of houses, the bushes and the plants

Are blanketed by the layers of snow

The ones who respect everything

About the intricacies of nature they know

Newness and cheerfulness

During the snowfall everyone begets

Harmonious sounds are in the air

When the snow melts

23. A DAY OF THE NATURAL WORLD

The sun is shining

The beautiful birds are in flight

Animals are grazing in the meadows

The snowy mountains are so bright

The butterflies and the bees are flying

Over the magnificent flowers and trees

A harmonious sound is in the air

Everyone can feel a gentle touch of the cool breeze

The splendor of rivers and waterfalls

Are imparting positive thoughts into one's mind

The lava is erupting from the volcanoes' craters

And imposing, man to be patient, sane, just, wise and kind

Nature is dancing
Nature is singing
Nature is blossoming
Nature is swinging

While the wind is blowing
Some leaves are swaying some are falling
To get affection, serenity, companionship and knowledge
Mother Earth is calling

24. AN ENLIGHTENING MESSAGE OF THE NATURAL JEWELS

When the sun goes down

The stars twinkle in the sky

Serenity and stillness are all around

They convey to you and I

One ought to believe in one's own self

One ought to enjoy each and every moment of this life

No one is here for long

One must avoid stress, strain and strife

One ought to spread love, peace and happiness

One ought to be positive

Take one's mind into a dimension

Where no thoughts exist those are negative

The mind is powerful

Utilize it well

Then one's whole life time

Will be nothing else but always swell

25. THE SPRING SEASON

When the rivers get their own pace

When the plants get their sheen

When the sun shines with intensity

When nature appears green

Birds and animals sing with a rhythmic sound

The splendor of Mother Earth, plants & creatures enhance

After hibernating, new creatures are all around

At that moment, it seems as though the trees & the bushes dance

All beings are unique, some are native, others exotic

Diversity and verity it shows

Positivity & reverence

For other beings within the self it grows

During this season

Water flows in a mystical way

The message of amore, tranquility, harmony & the union

The world receives on any spring day

Nature is full of colours

And sweet fragrance is far and wide

Mother Earth looks as though it's a marvelous painting

And each being enjoys & celebrates the spring season's joyride

26. APPROACHING SUMMER

When the sun shines with glory

Then the snow melts in the mountains

And the blowing wind is warm

The sky is always clear

It is the coming summer season's alarm

27. THE SUMMER SEASON

The surface is dry
And the temperature is high

The level of water is low
All life forms seek water, the Zebra, the Lion & the Crow

To save themselves from the heat wave
Hiding under bushes & trees, for shadows they crave

Some hide inside caves
Each one quiet, none raves

When the gentle breeze blows at dawn and dusk
With joy 'n' exhalation they brusque

28. EARLY RAINS

When the maiden rain of the rainy season comes

The natural seems to be reborn

It seems as though the creatures play the drums

Thus a rhythmical music goes on

All creatures feel the coolness, full of freshness with pleasure

Because hot days have gone

29. THE RAINY SEASON

New plants grow

And nature appears lush green

The rivers flow with an energetic pace

Mother Earth has a pleasant & a mysterious sheen

In nature, mystical sounds always exist

Most of the time, It rains here & there

The mist plays a game of hide and seek

Different native & exotic creatures appear

Animals and birds gather in the Great Plains

Amore & tranquility make the day

The Paddy is in the fields

From negative thoughts, this panorama takes everyone away

The surface becomes wet due to consistent rain

Nature conveys to everyone to be sane, just & kind

And the shepherds are in the mountains

The greenery encourages everyone to look deep into one's mind

In some places flood, soil- erosion and more
Unfathomable disasters take place
Home, wealth and lives are destroyed
Happiness and sorrow during the rains one can trace

Nature always gives the power
To accomplish one's vision
Nature comes with new lives
And it happens during the rainy season

When it rains
The mystical & rhythmical sounds start
Each & every being feels the beauty of this season
Each within its own heart

30. AN INVITATION OF AUTUMN

When falling leaves blow with the wind & are in flight

Falling all over the surface of Planet Earth

It seems as though

Mother Earth is like a bed of vibrantcolours

Nature calls

All living beings

To get the aroma of love, peace and companionship

It shows the realities of life

What all depends on

What one sees or observes or realizes

To comprehend

And open one's mind & vision

Everyone is invited

By 'The autumn season'

31. OH! WINTER

Oh! Winter, Oh! Winter

When you come

The shepherds leave the mountains

And move downhill due to the snow

Oh! Winter, Oh! Winter

When you come

The chant of fortune, adoration, coolness, serenity & glee

Nature and beautiful creatures always hum

Oh! Winter, Oh! Winter

When you come

The mountains are abound with snow

The cool breeze blows & water has a gentle flow

Oh! Winter, Oh! Winter

When you come

Many creatures hibernate

Like silvery pearls, nature glows in the moonlight

Oh! Winter, Oh! Winter

When you come

The valleys are covered by fog

It seems as though

You are going to narrate Mother Earth's travelogue

32. THE VOICE OF NATURE

Everyone shares with me

One's sorrow and happiness

Everyone feels the tranquility within me

I impart strength, courage & sweetness to all beings

In my surroundings

The writers and poets write about the realities of life

I sing the songs of love, enlightenment & respect

I always give everyone good vibrations

I always convey this message to the world

To eradicate negative thoughts

To live joyfully & peacefully

Love, respect & care for each & every being

Some worship me

On the other hand

Because of greed and wheeling-dealing

Some hurt me

Even though

I always give everyone

Serenity, happiness and heal

I impart the energy to become strong & positive

The flora & fauna are a part & parcel of me

I turn any spot into a beautiful place

The world is nourished by me

The glory of the world is enhanced by me

I'm nature

33. THE WISDOM OF A MOONLIT NIGHT

Beneath the sky

Glow-worms fly over trees and roses

The lakes, the rivers and the oceans seem like mirrors

When the moon comes with different phases and poses

This scenario inspires one and all

To introspect and conquer one's mind

To make one's surroundings healthy and green

And to be sane and kind

34. THE ENLIGHTENING MESSAGE OF MOTHER EARTH

Those beings who are in pain

The world ought to mend their woes and strengthen them

Those who have no food

The world ought to provide it to them

Those who have no education

The world ought to educate them

Those who have no habitat

The world ought to make shelters for them

Those who destroy the natural

The world ought to hinder & halt them

Those who contaminate nature

The world ought to stop them

Those who have given up on life & living

The world ought to lift & assist them

Those who destroy the ecology, the flora & fauna

The world ought to stop them

Those who are in need of assistance

The world ought to assist them

Those who are blind to realities & unable to tackle them

The world ought to show the right path & enlighten them
Those who spread envy, violence, negative vibes and extremism
The world ought to plant seeds of positivity to alter their mindset

35. A CALL OF THE NATURAL JEWELS

Experience

Newness, strength, courage

And loveliness within nature

It is expressed by

The enlightening ambiance of the natural

The welcoming gentle breeze

The moving leaves

The flowing rivers

The birds in flight

And the dancing trees

36. I'M EARTH

I'm Earth

You are my children

You call yourselves human beings

But you are usually inhuman

You destroy me

You contaminate me

Your negative intensions I can feel and see

You try to find new ways to hurt me

You excavate everything beyond requirements out of me

Why do you become evil?

And do such horrendous deeds?

Is it because of an unhealthy state of mental affairs, desires & greed?

And you are self centric, indulgent and take beyond your need

By comprehending your actions

I must say

Your mind is stuffed with negativity

Please transform

To make Planet Earth a better place to live in

Think about this for a while

What you are trying to be

Why you have forgotten that

I nourish and love you

I give you indispensable things

I impart you adoration, prosperity & happiness

I make your life flourishing and bright

I spread the fragrance of beautiful flowers

With my touch, you get courage and powers

Wake up Oh! My children wake up please

Don't hurt me more

Make the environment healthy and green

Be clear and calm in your mind

Take decisive actions

Recognize and eradicate sinful thought circuits

To nullify resultant sinful actions

Eradicate the evil that over powers you

And don't ignore your responsibilities & onus

Unity and cooperation bring serenity & healthy vibrations

Unite and co-operate

Otherwise negative vibrations, unfathomable disasters & weird mental illnesses

Will be forever the world's fate

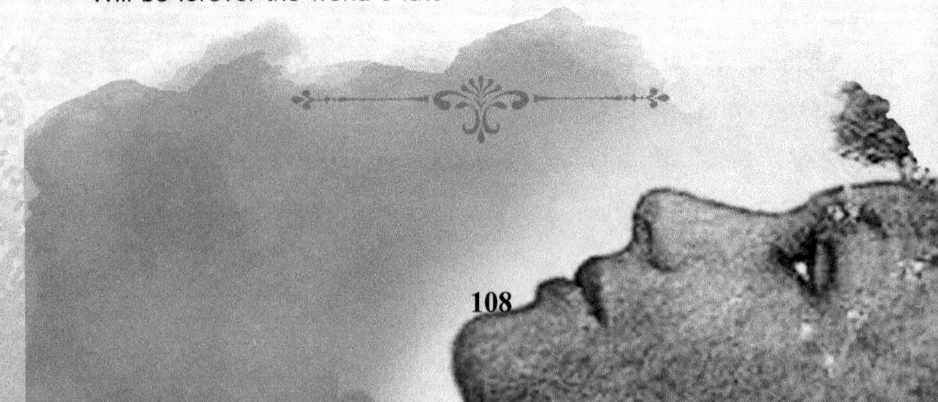

37. THE MESSAGE OF THE NATURAL WORLD

Nature conveys to everyone

The importance

Of abundant patience, unity & co-operation,

Love, respect & serenity

Freshness, companionship & the power of belief

And to be sane, just, civil & kind

The tree conveys to everyone

Give the best service to the world

Be polite

Be responsible

Spread goodwill

Encourage others to open their own mind

The mountains convey to everyone

Be brave and never give up

Neither be full of hate nor have any arrogance

Be a protector & don't be a destroyer

Have a compassionate heart

Don't be inane, insane, cruel, brutal & unkind

The stars convey to everyone

Lift and assist other lives

And help to make their lives

Prosperous, pleasant & serene

About their internal powers, potentials & abilities

One ought to, them remind

The lake and the moon convey to everyone

Become stable and calm

Introspect and rectify dark spots

Cleanse one's own self

And heal the world's woes

Be unfeigned & refined

The sun conveys to everyone

Be honest and punctual

Get the might from the universe

The past is dead & gone

Live in the 'Now'

Lethargy and negative thoughts one ought to leave behind

Birds convey to everyone

Enjoy and celebrate each & every moment

And don't harm anyone

Spread positive & healthy vibrations, harmony & happiness

Nothing is achievable

For the one who is negative, self centric & unrefined

The waterfalls, the oceans & the rivers convey to everyone

Time waits for none

Keep observing and learning and don't stop

Get the energy & get the light

And make the world flourishing and bright

Life is a blessing in itself and utterly wonderful, bear in mind

38. AN AWAKENING CALL

I nourish the world

Day and night

I make the world

Flourishing and bright

I always impart the massage which says

Respect all beings and nature

Don't try to hurt them

Follow the way of love and positivity

Eradicate evil powers and cruelty

Serve the world, your surroundings and relationships

Fulfill your responsibilities

Remember that

You are one of the beautiful creations

Of the universal powers

I'm your Mother 'TELLUS'

Turn me into the land of flowers

39. THE WORLD OF TODAY

The world is blatantly spreading

Poisonous smoke in the air

On the surface

Garbage, rot and squalor are here and there

The places of other beings are being occupied

Where they live and play

The rivers, the mountains & more are being contaminated

Such is the world's inane & insane way

The flora & fauna are being exterminated

Due to which most are nearly extinct or have disappeared

Immense buildings are covering the landscape

New problems are erupting, a lot of hindrances have appeared

The world is ignoring responsibilities

The world is continuously indulging in such deeds

The world has become so blind

Due to selfishness, avarice, unachievable desires and needs

40. WHY???

Oh! My dear children

Why are you destroying nature?

Oh! My dear children

Why are you striving to hurt or kill every creature?

Oh! My dear children

Why are you cutting down plants & trees?

Oh! My dear children

Why are you poisoning sweet water, fertile soil & the breeze?

Oh! My dear children

Why are you destroying other beings' homes?

Oh! My dear children

Why are you making lethal weapons and bombs?

Oh! My dear children

Why are you polluting the surface?

Oh! My dear children

Why are you mining on my face?

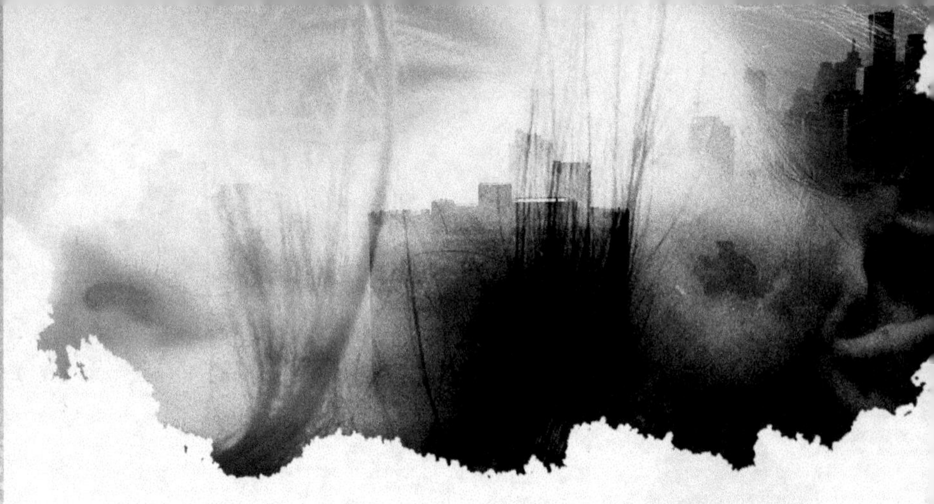

Oh! My dear children

Why are you allowing toxic emissions of factories & mills?

Oh! My dear children

Why are you breaking down the mountains, the boulders & the hills?

Oh! My dear children

Why are you making the environment filthy, unhealthy & unclear?

Oh! My dear children

Why are you spreading poisonous gases in the air?

Slowly and steadily due to your vicious actions

I'm dying, losing the greenery & becoming a filthy barren land

Oh! My dear children

When will you understand?

Accept the fact that you have created imbalance

It's never too late

Love, peace, tranquility, prosperity and healthy vibes

To make your fate

Plant trees, eradicate the cruelty within you

Don't spread poisonous gases & don't make weapons & bombs

Protect & preserve all species, ecology and flora & fauna

And don't eradicate other beings' homes

In case you don't

The world will become barren and mutant

Many life forms and beings will become extinct

Then I'll see you repent

41. THE VOICE OF THE OTHER BEINGS

We live

On the surface & in the oceans

We never harm Mother Earth

But human beings strive to hurt our emotions

We make our home in the forests & caves

Over & under the trees & below gigantic waves

We spread the message of affection, amity and tranquility

Through our vibrations

We fly in the sky

We run and play on the surface

We serve the world without any break

We enjoy swimming in the seas, rivers & lakes

Oh! Humans

Let's enjoy & celebrate this life

And its each & every moment as well

In the mysterious world

Don't create stress, strain & strife

Don't hurt & kill us

We don't do harm to anyone

We live in our own world peacefully & happily

Incase you don't stop

We will become extinct

With no trace of us far and wide

Oh! Humans

Without us

Life is not possible

Please realize

Keeping us safe & sound is only sane & wise

42. OH! DEAR CHILDREN

Oh! Dear children

When you keep me

Healthy & prosperous

Beautiful & clean

I feel exhilarated

By my lush green

Oh! Dear Children

When you serve other beings

Those who are in stress, strain & strife

And spread positivity in their lives

I feel so delighted

It shows in my sheen

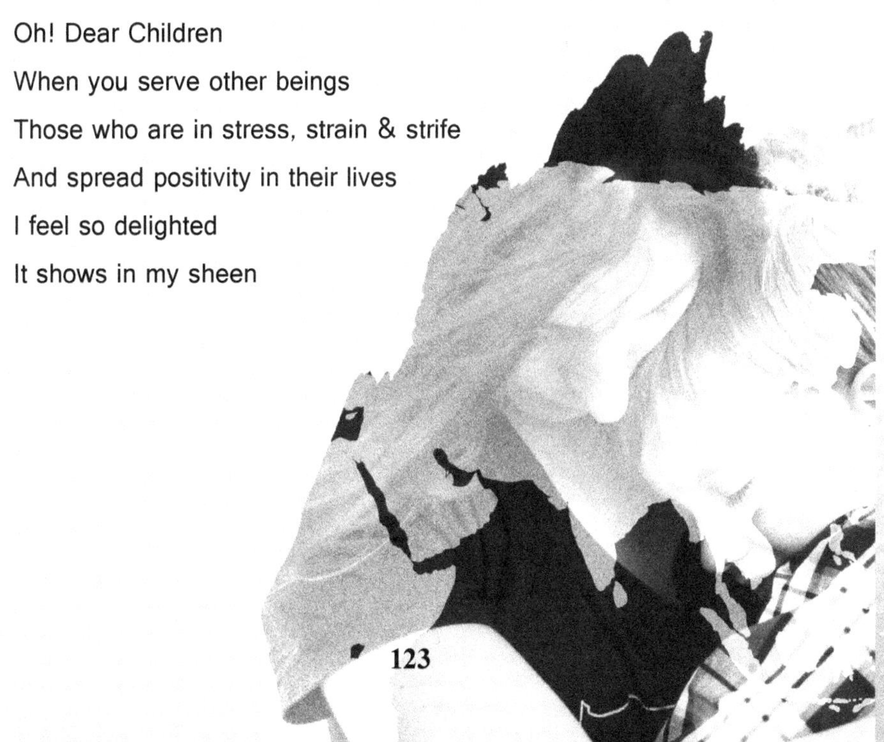

Oh! Dear children

When you feed any other being

And give them a place to live

Those who have no habitat & nothing to eat

Upon seeing your zeal & positive approach towards life

I feel wondrous

And create a marvelous scene

Oh! Dear children

You protest and fight

With the system or the world

When sinful deeds take place

Like exploiting somebody's birth right

I feel charmed

When you are not an ignominious has-been

Oh! Dear children

When you show the right path

To those who are blind to realities & unable to tackle them

And inspire them to be self −reliant

I feel joyful

Cause 'The Pure' while seeking knowledge & wisdom, doesn't have

to glean

Oh! Dear children

When those who face brutality & seek justice

You fight to attain, what is due to them

And stop these atrocious acts

I feel blissful

Because you fight for right, absolutely keen

Oh! Dear children

When you lift & help persons to reach their destinations

When you spread the message of love, tranquility & unity

While respecting all beings

I feel wonderful

Young and lean

Oh! Dear children

When you show a positive attitude towards other beings

And give them exposure of other dimensions & the cycle of life as well

And Plant seeds of positivity in their mind-space

I feel gracious

When you know the self and your mien

Oh! Dear children

When you nullify the dark spots within you

And love care & respect for things around you

My heart blossoms

With happiness and freshness

I feel peaceful

Because you comprehend what I mean

126

43. LET'S DO IT TODAY & NOW

During the winter season, when the mist comes

It seems as though the mountains disappear

When the mist vanishes

The mountain peaks covered with snow re-appear

At that moment nature appears incredible

Freshness, positive vibes, joy, tranquility & love are in the air

Knowledge and wisdom of Mother Earth

The snowy peaks of the mountains also share

Now the world is in the 21st century

Man's avarice has invited many problems like Global warming

No actions, only talks take place everyday

In tandem, the world is exhausting her natural resources & it harming

The way the world is mis-utilizing the natural resources

And poisoning, harming & destroying Mother Earth

The day is not far away when mist and snow will not be there

After that the world will comprehend their true worth

Let's strive to maintain the mountains' sheen

And must achieve it somehow

Let's not wait for tomorrow

Let's be sane & do it today & now

44. OH! MY DEAR CHILDREN

Oh! My dear children

Why are you destroying me due to inane attraction of your greed?

I'm your Mother Earth

Who always fulfills your need?

Oh! My dear children

Why are you incarcerating nature inside the cages?

How can you forget that?

Nature has been nourishing you since ages

Oh! My dear children

Why are you spreading brutality & hate?

How can you forget that?

Love, friendship, prosperity, brotherhood & unity, is your fate

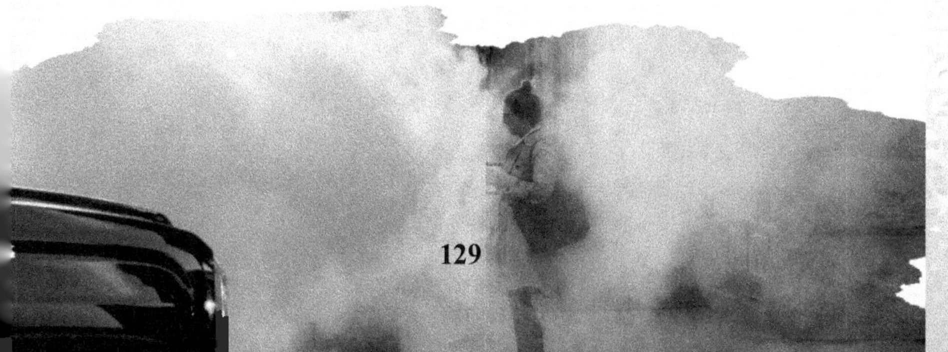

The forests, the mountains, the rivers, the surface and the sky

Why are you eradicating their beauty?

How can you forget that?

To make the world healthy & green, serve all beings, is your duty

Oh! My dear children

Unite and co-operate to make me healthy & clean

Spread glee & protect the flora & fauna

And make me utterly wonderful & green

45. THE SAYINGS OF THE WISE PEOPLE

Wise people say

Life is a precious chance

To serve & enjoy

To read & write

To sing & dance

To feel loveliness, newness and serenity

In the sun's domain

Pleasure is one's birthright during one's life time

Life is just like the leaves of trees that come and wither away

One ought to embrace nature

To be able to accomplish one's onus

And save natural resources for the next generations to come

Because these priceless resources will not be there anymore

Unless one protects and maintains the natural

Instead of greedily or aimlessly destroying Planet Earth

46. THE SORROW OF THE NATURAL WORLD AND WISE CALLING

While observing the state of affairs of our world

Mother Earth is in pain

Some inane & inhuman beings usually destroy rare & priceless things

Lacking healthy intensions & shirking onus, acts of the insane

The agony of sane beings endured in silence

Mother Earth hears them screaming

To turn Mother Earth into hell

Evil powers are scheming

The lack of awareness, personal benefits and rapacity

Make them blind

They are forgetting, aren't accepting the fact

That Mother Earth is so caring and kind

Thus, they are polluting

The precious pearls of nature

They are exterminating

The beautiful plants and creatures

They are ignoring

The importance and rights of other beings

For them other beings are 'Milking cows'

That's why they keep clipping their wings

To Mother Earth's agony

The world ought to eradicate evil powers

The world ought to embellish

Mother Earth with beauty, grace & fragrant flowers

The world must be united

And spread the message of love, peace, happiness & prosperity

But if the world will be late

The fate of the world is envy, cruelty & brutality

47. RESPECT

Respect Mother Earth

Respect all beings

Don't try to hurt them

Impart love and cheerfulness

Don't forget what they do for us

Respect the trees and the forests

Respect the flowers and the plants

Don't crush or cut or pluck them

Plant them, make Mother Earth greener

Give devotion, tenderness and reverence

Don't forget what they do for us

Respect the mountains and the rivers

Respect the plains and the sky

Respect the flora & fauna

Don't contaminate and destroy them

Spread serenity, love and positivity

Neither ignore nor forget the fact

They are precious & priceless

48. WATER, THE PRICELESS RESOURCE

Water is mighty

Water gives life

When it flows in the magnificent rivers, waterfalls & oceans

It heals stress & strain thus one tends to avoid strife

When water flows

The songs of enlightenment it always sings

It shows the path

Be sane, wise & kind, never clip anyone's wings

Water conveys to the world

About the significance of time

Water expresses emotions through it's sounds

And helps everyone back into rhyme

Water makes the world

Prosperous and wealthy

And water helps to make Mother Earth

Green and healthy

Water nourishes the world

Water is pure

Water is a healer

Water has a unique lure

As one sows so one reaps

Water always indicates

The mysteries of the universe

Water possesses & states

On the other hand

The world contaminates water

The world ignores& forgets certain facts, water is a blessing in itself

And imparts the energy to every being like man, fish & otter

Water enhances

The exquisiteness of Mother Earth

The world ought to comprehend

Its true worth

The world ought to preserve its sources

Otherwise Mother Earth will lose her greenery

Everyone will repent & lament

After seeing Mother Earth's pathetically barren scenery

To save water

The world ought to maintain its sources

The world ought to unite & cooperate

To preserve its resources

49. INTROSPECT

Observe your own thoughts & actions

Think about this for a while

What you are trying to be

And the deeds you have done

Have a positive attitude in life

Don't hurt any being anymore

Be serious about your responsibilities

Since it's your onus

Don't think that

Hurting any being is entertainment or fun

50. SAVE WATER SAVE LIFE

Look at sweet water

Because of inhuman actions

The beauty and purity of it

Has become pathetically unhealthy and worse

Look at sweet water

Inside it, there is usually muck and mud

Every day

The world is contaminating water without care

The world is wasting it

The world is destroying sweet water's sources

Save sweet water and its sources

Otherwise, water will be the cause of the next war or strife

Planet Earth will become unproductive

No one will be alive

Don't contaminate & waste sweet water

Don't destroy its priceless sources

Let's unite to clean and save sweet water

It ought to be our dream

To make our blue planet healthy and save its sources

We ought to work like a team

51. THE MESSAGE FROM THE NATURAL

Mother Earth is so beautiful

Mother Earth has a glorious grace

Mother Earth is so wonderful

Mother Earth gives everyone a deep embrace

Mother Earth is incredible

Mother Earth nourishes all beings

Mother Earth is amazing

The songs of love, serenity, joyous & enlightenment she sings

Mother Earth contributes a lot to living beings

On the other hand, inane people destroy her sheen

Our world can reciprocate with respect and love

Let's strive to maintain her greenery & keep her clean

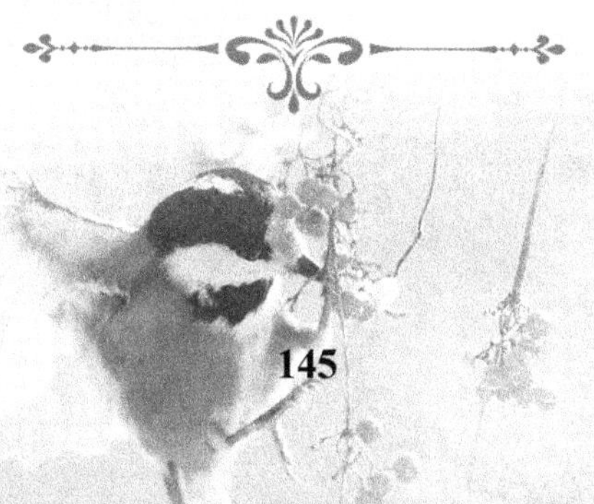

52. THE CALL OF NATURE

Please don't hurt animals and birds
Let's give them love and respect
Let's let them be lively
Please don't indulge in any inane & insane act

Please don't forget that
A melody of affection, companionship & serenity, they always sing
Please don't forget that
They have equal rights similar to each and every human being

Please don't forget that
They make the world flourishing and bright
Please don't forget that
Their appearances turn nature into a wondrous sight

Please don't forget that
They make the world magnificent & wealthy
Please don't forget that
They make the environment incredible & healthy

Please don't forget that

Their verities are so many

They are so innocent

They aren't harmful or zany

Please don't forget that

They never spread jealousy or hate

Please don't forget that

They make Mother Earth like a marvelous portrait

Please don't capture or kill them

For your greed and pleasure

Please don't forget that

They are Mother Earth's precious treasure

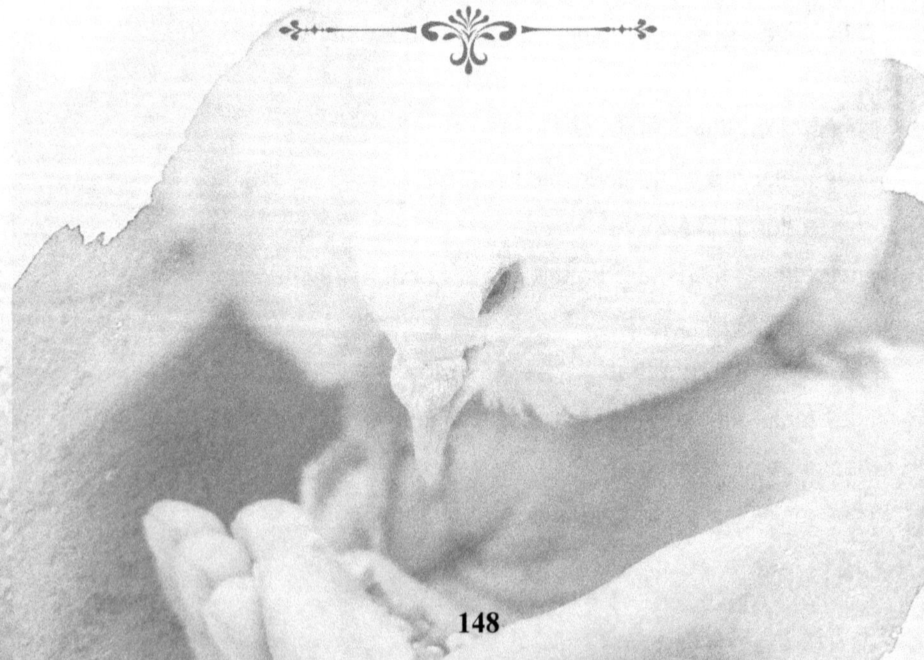

53. LET'S UNITE

Let's unite to give Mother Earth love and respect

Let's unite to learn from our mistakes of the past

Let's unite to protect the flora & fauna

It's time to act to save our Global Village, really fast

Let's unite to make Mother Earth healthy and green

It ought to be our dream

It's achievable

We ought to work, like a team

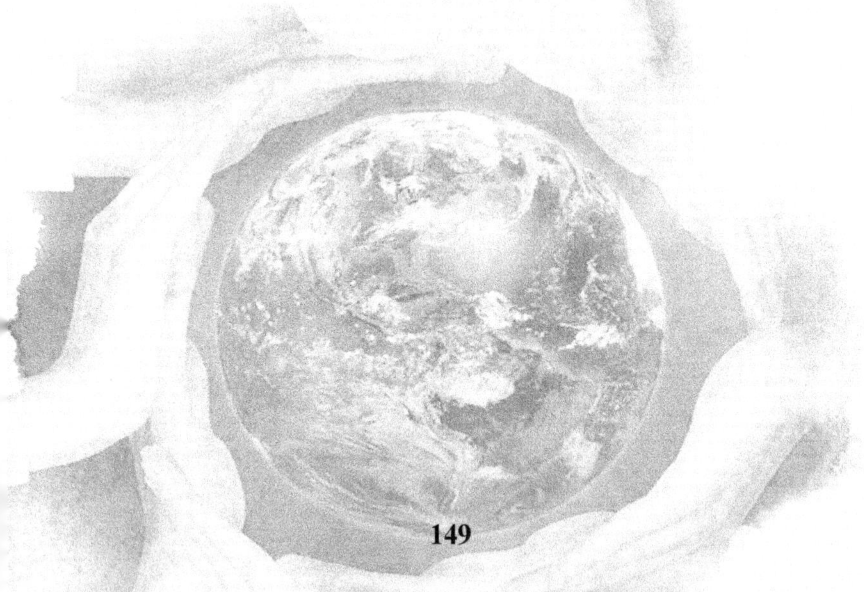

54. UNITY AND CO-OPERATION

Unity and co-operation

Bring serenity, prosperity, and positive vibrations

Unity and co-operation

Turn pathetic conditions into healthy situations

Unity and co-operation

Bring love and happiness

Unity and co-operation

Make strong relationship & impart peacefulness

Unity and co-operation

Heal various woes

The change forthe positive is achievable through unity & co-operation

Nature conveys to us every day since she knows

Thus we ought to unite and co-operate

To plant more trees or else of them there will be no trace

We ought to unite and co-operate

To make Mother Earth a green & a beautiful place

We ought to change the mindset of those people

Whose mental state of affairs is not well

We ought to take decisive actions to negate

Those who are trying to transform Mother Earth into hell

We must make Mother Earth prosperous and bright

We have to start it now

This vision is achievable

We have to accomplish it somehow

Otherwise Planet Earth will be eerily quiet and barren

The creatures, the plants and the trees will not be there

Planet Earth will have the leftover weapons & immense ruins

And have a poisoned atmosphere everywhere

55. GIVE A HAND

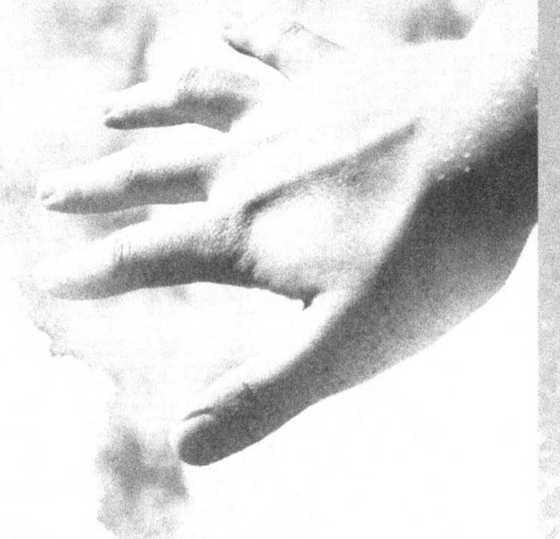

Give a hand

To protect each and every being

Give a hand

To make Mother 'TELLUS' Greener

Give a hand

To plant trees

Give a hand

To save the world from global warming and associated problems

Give a hand

To destroy evil powers

Give a hand

To spread good vibrations

Give a hand

To stop violence, riots, terrorism and horrendous deeds

Give a hand

To stop pollution

Give a hand

To cure and eradicate terrible diseases

Give a hand

To stop the world from destroying nature

Give a hand

It's never too late

Give a hand

To make unity, prosperity, love & friendship our fate

56. I, I, I & I

I, I, I & I try to win over nature

I try to kill & incarcerate creatures

I try to occupy other beings' land

I try to destroy this blue Planet

On the other hand

I always feel and claim that

I'm sane, wise, just, reasonable & civilized

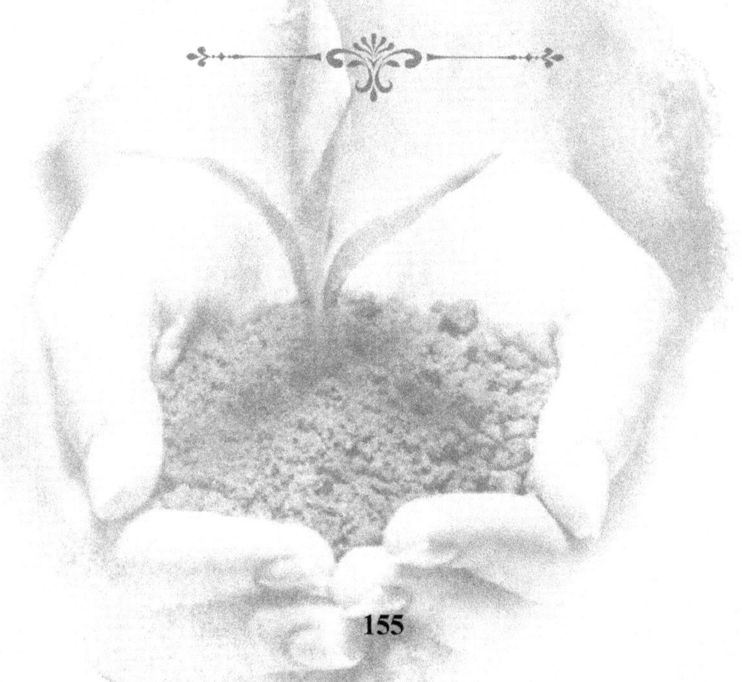

Everything is within
Don't seek answers of your queries outside
Ask your soul

www.ingramcontent.com/pod-product-compliance
Lightning Source LLC
LaVergne TN
LVHW051222200726

843510LV00011B/1454